FREE MASK

You Will Need:

- Thin elastic, wool or string
- Scissors
- Sticky Tape

Instructions:

1. Pull out the mask page.
2. Pop out the mask.
3. Cut enough elastic/wool/string to fit around the back of your head.
4. Attach to the back of the mask with some sticky tape.
5. Have fun with your new mask!

SCISSORS ARE SHARP! ASK AN ADULT FOR HELP BEFORE USING.

CONTENTS

INTENDED FOR MATURE AUDIENCES

CARTMAN

MEGATRON

Pedigree® Published 2013.
Pedigree Books Limited, Beech Hill House, Walnut Gardens, Exeter, Devon EX4 4DH
www.pedigreebooks.com | books@pedigreegroup.co.uk

STAN

LIKES
KYLE.
CANADIAN TV STARS TERRANCE AND PHILLIP.
DISLIKES
ERIC.

DISTINGUISHING CHARACTERISTICS
BOBBLE HAT. TENDENCY TO VOMIT
IN FEMALE COMPANY.
MOST LIKELY TO SAY
"THIS IS PRETTY F***ED UP
RIGHT HERE."
LEAST LIKELY TO SAY
ANYTHING FOR VERY LONG WITHOUT
SWEARING.
AKA
TOOL SHED

STAN IS ABOUT THE ONLY NORMAL PERSON IN SOUTH PARK. THAT IS, IF ANYONE CAN BE DESCRIBED AS NORMAL WHEN THEY HAVE THE LIKES OF KENNY AND ERIC AS FRIENDS, AND WHEN THEY LIVE IN A CRAZY PLACE LIKE SOUTH PARK.

KYLE

LIKES
STAN
(THEY ARE BEST FRIENDS).
DISLIKES
ERIC, HIS OVERBEARING MOTHER
(ON OCCASION).
ANTI-SEMITISM
(ESPECIALLY FROM ERIC).

DISTINGUISHING CHARACTERISTICS
GREEN HAT. JEWISHNESS.
MOST LIKELY TO SAY
"GODDAMN IT CARTMAN!"
LEAST LIKELY TO SAY
"WELL SAID ERIC! I AGREE."
AKA
THE HUMAN KITE

DESPITE HAVING THE MOTHER FROM HELL IN SHEILA *BROFLOVSKI*, *KYLE*, ONE OF THE TOWN'S FEW JEWISH RESIDENTS IS RELATIVELY NORMAL TOO. LITTLE WONDER HE'S REMAINED STAN'S BEST FRIEND FOR SO LONG AND OFTEN REMAINS THE ONLY SOURCE OF COMMON SENSE AND REASON AMONGST THE GROUP.

CARTMAN

LIKES
HIMSELF, FOOD, HIS MOM,
PET CAT MR. KITTY.
ACTOR MEL GIBSON.

DISLIKES
HIPPIES,
KYLE,
MOST THINGS.

DISTINGUISHING CHARACTERISTICS
FAT, NOISY, FOUL-MOUTHED
OBNOXIOUS SPOILT BRAT.

MOST LIKELY TO SAY
"DON'T CALL ME BITCH, BITCH!"

LEAST LIKELY TO SAY
"THERE AREN'T ENOUGH
HIPPIES 'ROUND HERE."

AKA
THE COON

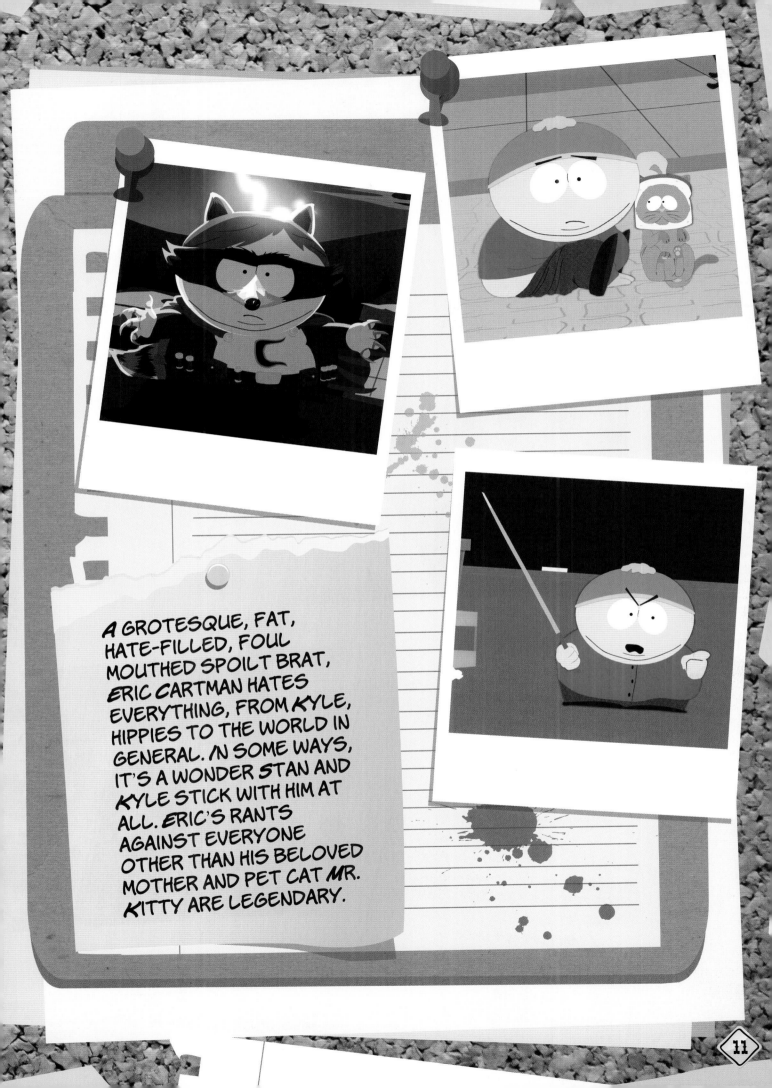

A GROTESQUE, FAT, HATE-FILLED, FOUL MOUTHED SPOILT BRAT, ERIC CARTMAN HATES EVERYTHING, FROM KYLE, HIPPIES TO THE WORLD IN GENERAL. IN SOME WAYS, IT'S A WONDER STAN AND KYLE STICK WITH HIM AT ALL. ERIC'S RANTS AGAINST EVERYONE OTHER THAN HIS BELOVED MOTHER AND PET CAT MR. KITTY ARE LEGENDARY.

KENNY

LIKES
GIRLS. WHEN HE CAN BE UNDERSTOOD, KENNY OFTEN SEEMS HIGHLY SEXUALLY CHARGED.

DISLIKES
ERIC.
DYING VIOLENTLY.

DISTINGUISHING CHARACTERISTICS
ORANGE COAT WHICH OBSCURES HIS MOUTH. TENDENCY TO DIE VIOLENTLY.

MOST LIKELY TO SAY
"MIFFURGMFFURGH!"

LEAST LIKELY TO SAY
ANYTHING COHERENT.

AKA
MYSTERION

KENNY IS ONE OF THOSE BOYS WHO HAS NO LUCK WHATSOEVER. RENDERED INCOMPREHENSIBLE BY HIS STIFLING COAT, HE IS ALSO ONE OF THE POOREST CHILDREN IN TOWN AND ALSO FAMOUSLY PRONE TO BOUTS OF SUDDEN, PREMATURE DEATH.

TIMMY

TIMMY IS ONE OF SOUTH PARK'S FEW DISABLED CHARACTERS AND HAS A VOCABULARY RESTRICTED TO JUST A FEW SHORT WORDS AND PHRASES. DESPITE THIS, TIMMY PLAYS SUCCESSFULLY WITH HIS OWN ROCK BAND, TIMMY AND THE LORDS OF THE UNDERWORLD!

LIKES
PERFORMING LIVE MUSIC.
DISLIKES
JIMMY, (AT LEAST, AT FIRST).
DISTINGUISHING CHARACTERISTICS
WHEELCHAIR-BOUND.
MOST LIKELY TO SAY
"TIMMEH! LIVIN' A LIE"
LEAST LIKELY TO SAY
MUCH ELSE.
AKA
IRON MAIDEN

14

JIMMY

SOUTH PARK'S ONLY OTHER DISABLED FOURTH GRADER (APART FROM TIMMY), JIMMY CAN SPEAK FREELY. IN FACT, HE SPEAKS A LITTLE TOO FREELY DEPLOYING HIS STAND-UP COMEDY ROUTINE SKILLS TO MAKE JOKES AT THE EXPENSE OF OTHER SOUTH PARK RESIDENTS.

LIKES
COMEDY.

DISLIKES
NOTHING, OBVIOUSLY.

DISTINGUISHING CHARACTERISTICS
USES CRUTCHES

MOST LIKELY TO SAY
"WOW! WHAT A GREAT AUDIENCE!" ALSO OFTEN ENDS SENTENCES BY SAYING: "VERY MUCH."

LEAST LIKELY TO SAY
NOTHING. HE RARELY SHUTS UP.

BIG GAY AL

BIG GAY AL IS – AS HIS NAME SUGGESTS – SOUTH PARK'S GAYEST RESIDENT. INDEED, HE MIGHT ACTUALLY BE THE GAYEST MAN WHO HAS EVER LIVED. HE IS ALSO GENUINELY NICE AND RUNS BIG GAY AL'S BIG GAY ANIMAL SANCTUARY.

LIKES
MEN.

DISLIKES
CHRISTIANS, REPUBLICANS AND NAZIS.

DISTINGUISHING CHARACTERISTICS
INCREDIBLE LEVELS OF CAMPNESS.
FLAMBOYANT DRESS SENSE.

MOST LIKELY TO SAY
"I'M SUPER, THANKS FOR ASKING!"

LEAST LIKELY TO SAY
"WHOA! CHECK IT OUT DUDES! TOTALLY
HOT CHICK UP AHEAD, SIX O CLOCK!"

ACT OUT
SOUTH PARK GAY MEN'S
ADVOCATES

BUTTERS

BUTTERS IS THE MOST INNOCENT OF THE *SOUTH PARK* CREW. PERPETUALLY PERKY AND FAR LESS PRONE TO FOUL LANGUAGE THAN THE OTHER CHILDREN, HIS NAIVETY AND GULLIBILITY, THOUGH ENDEARING, MAKE HIM VULNERABLE TO PRANKS AND UNWITTING PARTICIPATION IN *CARTMAN'S* SCHEMES.

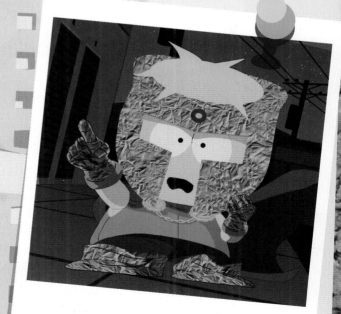

LIKES
LIFE. BUTTERS EVEN FINDS BEAUTY IN SADNESS.
DISLIKES
THE BAD THINGS THAT FREQUENTLY BEFALL HIM
DISTINGUISHING CHARACTERISTICS
HAPPY GO LUCKY ATTITUDE.
MOST LIKELY TO SAY
"OH HAMBURGERS!"
LEAST LIKELY TO SAY
"**** THAT."

EVENTS

Communi

HEY FELLAS!

HEY, BUTTERS.

EVENTS

BOY, AM I GLAD TO SEE YOU GUYS! THERE'S LOTS OF KIDS HERE FROM OTHER SCHOOLS. I DON'T KNOW ANYBODY!

ALL RIGHT, BOYS, WE'RE GONNA HEAD TO THE BAR. WE'LL BE BACK TO PICK YOU UP AT NINE.

YOU BOYS JUST MAKE SURE TO OBEY THE *SCOUT LEADER*, NOW. HE'S THE MAN IN CHARGE!

SCOTCH

♪ HELLOOooo ♪ SCOUTS!

ENTRANCE

SCOTCH

HEY! IT'S BIG GAY AL!

TIMMEH!!!

YOU WERE RIGHT, DAD! SCOUTS IS **AWESOME!**

WE TOLD **GHOST STORIES** AND LEARNED HOW TO MAKE A **TORNADO** IN A GLASS BOTTLE!

YEAH, AND WE LEARNED HOW TO MAKE **CAKES** AND **MUFFINS** FOR OUR BAKE SALE!

AND BEST OF ALL, WE MET THIS KID NAMED **JIMMY!**

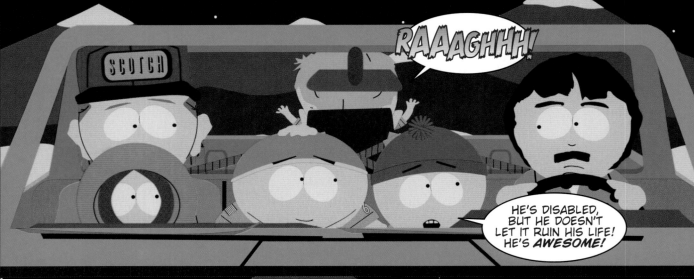

RAAAGHHH!

HE'S DISABLED, BUT HE DOESN'T LET IT RUIN HIS LIFE! HE'S **AWESOME!**

YEAH! WE'RE GONNA USE HIM TO HELP RAISE MONEY AT OUR BAKE SALE.

CARTMAN, DON'T SAY "USE HIM", YOU **BIG SILLY GOOSE!**

SCREEECHHH!!!

WHAT DID YOU SAY?!

I JUST... CALLED CARTMAN A NAME. HE'S BEING A SILLY GOOSE!

OR GARRISON? "MR. HAT... BE *QUIET*, MR. HAT. HELLO THERE, CHILDREN. MR. HAT, MR. HAT..."

HA HAHAHA

HA HAHAHA

OR HOW 'BOUT *CHEF*? "I'M MAKIN' *SALISBURY STEAK* FOR LUNCH!"

CHEF

AND OF COURSE MY VERY FAVORITE...

"TIMMEH! TIMMEH!"

"I'M-LIVIN'-A-LIE... TIMMEH!"

HAHAHA

HAHAHA

HA HAHAHA

HA HAHAHA

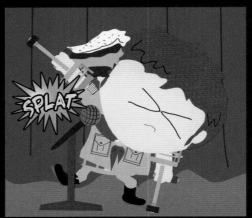

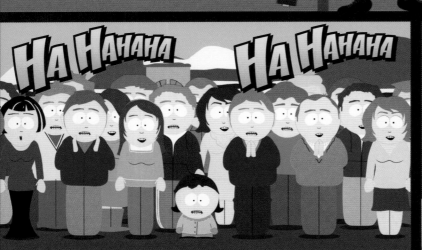

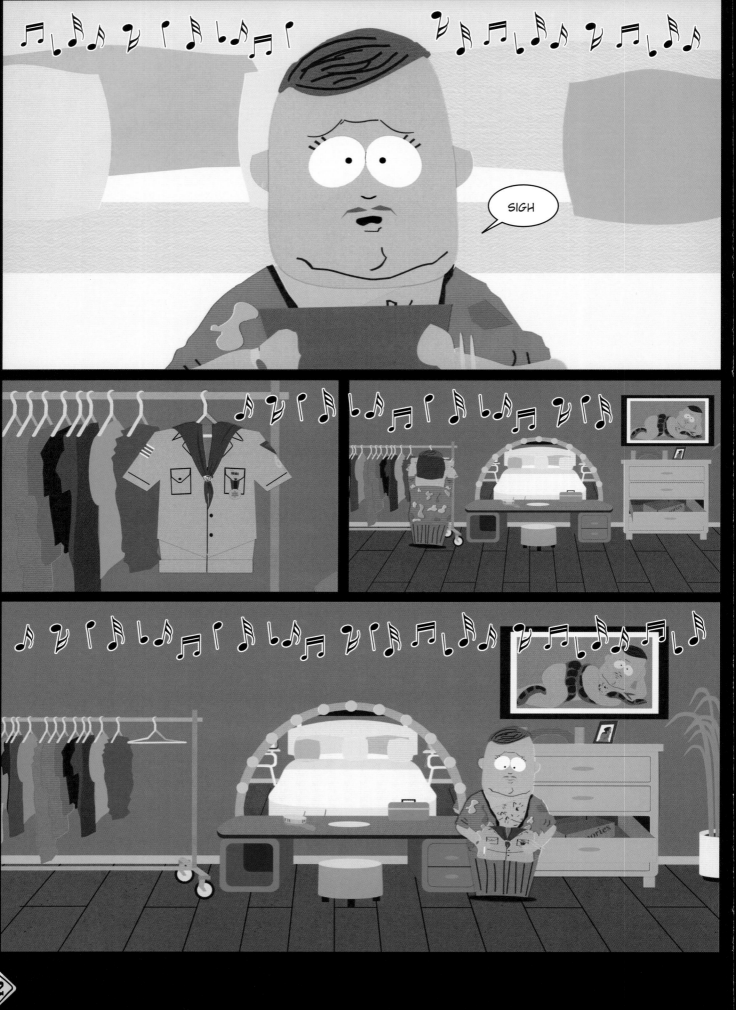

AND S-SO I SAYS TO HIM, "HEY I MAY BE H-HANDICAPPED, BUT I'M NOT *D-DEAF!*"

HA HAHAHA

WOW, WHAT A TERRIFIC AUDIENCE.

FOR MY NEXT JOKE, I'M GOING TO NEED A V-VOLUNTEER FROM THE AUDIENCE. H-HOW 'BOUT *YOU*, TIMMY?

TIMMEH...

SURE, COME ON UP HERE, TIM-TIM.

TIMMY, LADIES AND GENTLEMEN. LET'S ALL GIVE HIM A HAND, VERY MUCH.

HA HAHAHA

COME TO THINK OF IT, GIVE HIM A PAIR OF *LEGS,* TOO!

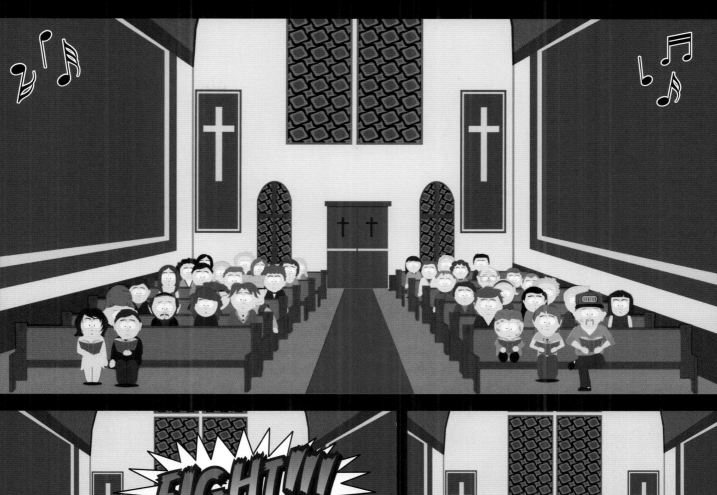

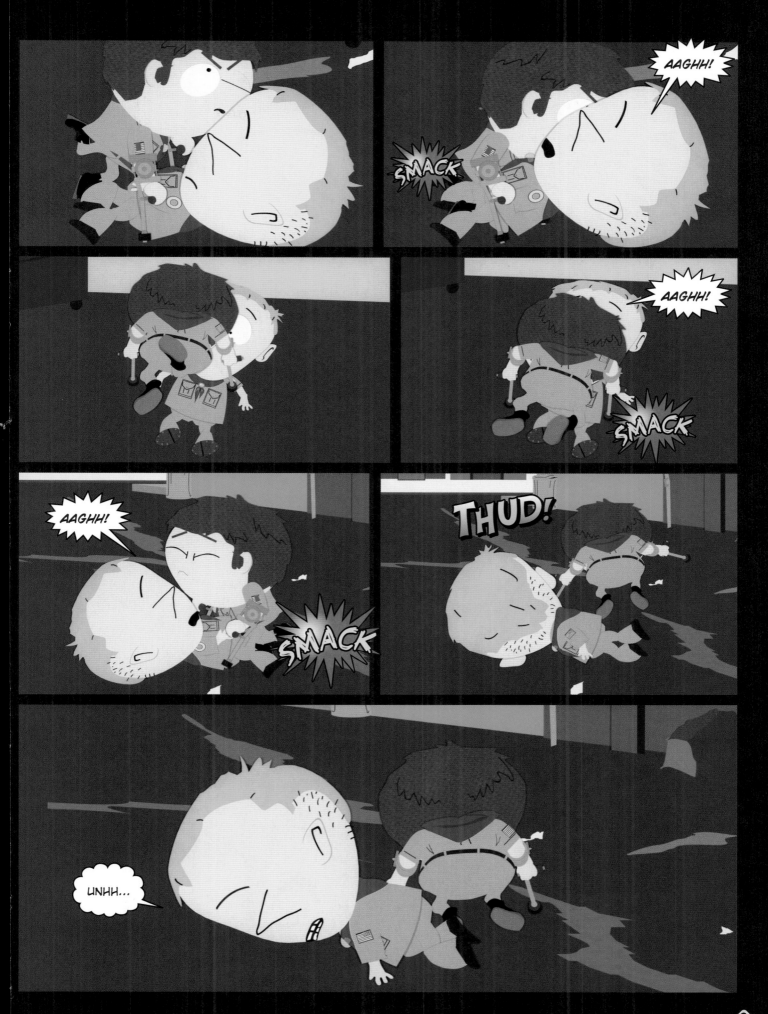

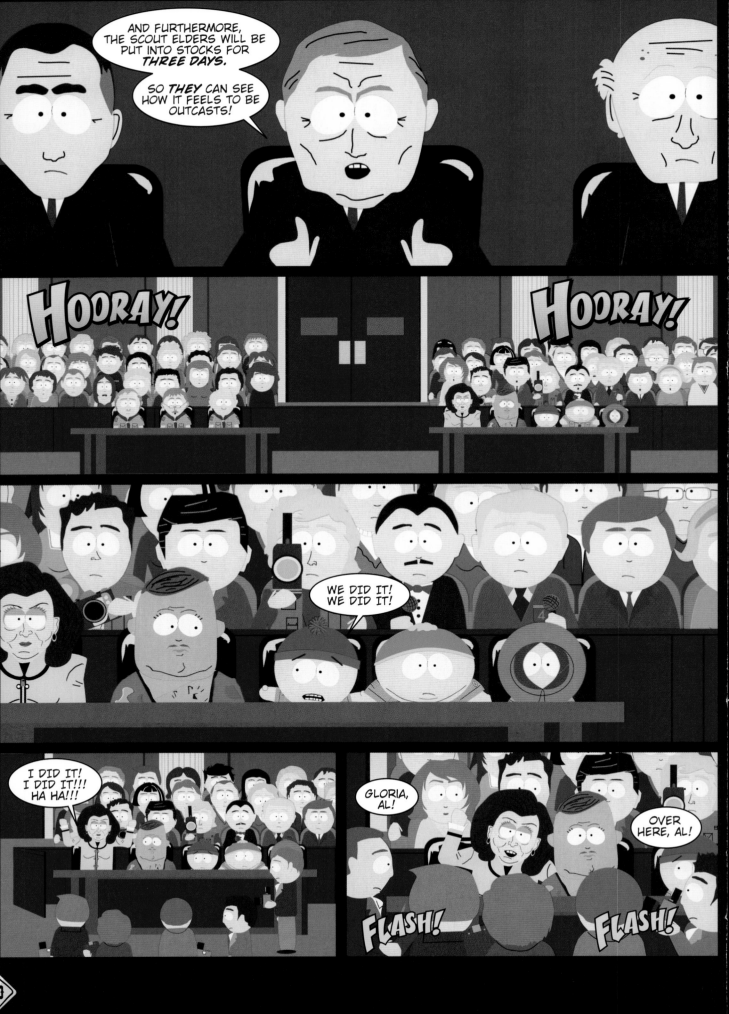

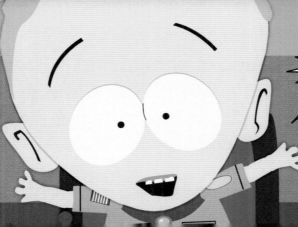

THE END!

South Park Annual 2014

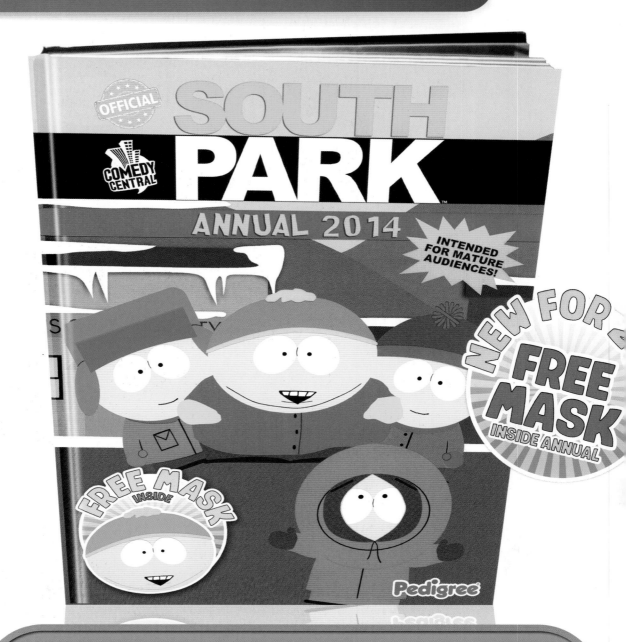

Visit **Pedigreebooks.com** to find out more
on this year's **South Park Annual**,
scan with your mobile device to learn more.

Visit www.pedigreebooks.com

Pedigree Books, Beech Hill House, Walnut Gardens, Exeter EX4 4DH